the Eye of
the Storm

JOB

by Bryson Smith

MATTHIAS MEDIA

The Eye of the Storm
© Matthias Media, 1999

Published in the UK by
THE GOOD BOOK COMPANY
Elm House, 37 Elm Road
New Malden, Surrey KT3 3HB
Tel: 020-8942-0880
Fax: 020-8942-0990
e-mail: admin@thegoodbook.co.uk
Website: www.thegoodbook.co.uk

ISBN 1 876326 08 5

Cover Illustration: Liz Murphy

Contents

How to make the most of these studies

1. What is an Interactive Bible Study?

These 'interactive' Bible studies are a bit like a guided tour of a famous city. The studies will take you through the book of Job, pointing out things along the way, filling in background details, and suggesting avenues for further exploration. But there is also time for you to do some sight-seeing of your own—to wander off, have a good look for yourself, and form your own conclusions.

In other words, we have designed these studies to fall half-way between a sermon and a set of unadorned Bible study questions. We want to provide stimulation and input and point you in the right direction, while leaving you to do a lot of the exploration and discovery yourself.

We hope that these studies will stimulate lots of 'interaction'—interaction with the Bible, with the things we've written, with your own current thoughts and attitudes, with other people as you discuss them, and with God as you talk to him about it all.

2. The format

Each study contains sections of text to introduce, summarize, suggest and provoke. We've left plenty of room in the margins for you to jot comments and questions as you read. Interspersed throughout the text are three types of 'interaction', each with their own symbol:

For starters

Questions to break the ice and get you thinking.

Investigate

Questions to help you investigate key parts of the Bible.

Think it through

Questions to help you think through the implications of your discoveries and write down your own thoughts and reactions.

When you come to one of these symbols, you'll know that it's time to do some work of your own.

3. Suggestions for Individual Study

- Before you begin, pray that God would open your eyes to what he is saying in James and give you the spiritual strength to do something about it. You may be spurred to pray again at the end of the study.
- Work through the study, following the directions as you go. Write in the spaces provided.
- Resist the temptation to skip over the *Think it through* sections. It is important to think about the sections of text (rather than just accepting them as true) and to ponder the implications for your life. Writing these things down is a very valuable way to get your thoughts working.
- Take what opportunities you can to talk to others about what you've learnt.

4. Suggestions for Group Study

- Much of the above applies to group study as well. The studies are suitable for structured Bible study or cell groups, as well as for more informal pairs and threesomes. Get together with a friend/s and work through them at your own pace; use them as the basis for regular Bible study with your spouse. You don't need the formal structure of a 'group' to gain maximum benefit.

- It is *vital* that group members work through the study themselves *before* the group meets. The group discussion can take place comfortably in an hour (depending on how side-tracked you get!), but only if all the members have done the work and are familiar with the material.

- Spend most of the group time discussing the 'interactive' sections—*Investigate* and *Think it Through*. Reading all the text together will take too long and should be unnecessary if the group members have done their preparation. You may wish to underline and read aloud particular paragraphs or sections of text that you think are important.

- The role of the group leader is to direct the course of the discussion and to try to draw the threads together at the end. This will mean a little extra preparation—underlining important sections of text to emphasize, working out which questions are worth concentrating on, and being sure of the main thrust of the study. Leaders will also probably want to work out approximately how long they'd like to spend on each part.

- We haven't included an 'answer guide' to the questions in the studies. This is a deliberate move. We want to give you a guided tour of James not a lecture. There is more than enough in the text we have written and the questions we have asked to point you in what we think is the right direction. The rest is up to you.

Good times, Bad times

Workers dropped a crate containing a 75 million-year-old dinosaur skeleton outside a museum in the The Hague, Netherlands, breaking it into 188 pieces. "The two Canadian scientists who had spent two years gluing together the skeleton had tears in their eyes", a spokesman told *De Telegraph* reporter.
The Bulletin, October 7, 1997.

Most of us know what it's like to have one of those days. A day where nothing goes right and everything goes wrong. Sometimes those sorts of days are nothing more than a nuisance, and given time we can think back and laugh. Sometimes those days are far more tragic. The day the biopsy test comes back positive. The day the knock at the door is the police to tell you about a fatal accident. The day you discover a terrible secret within a relationship. These are days which can be the start of unimaginable grieving and suffering.

The Old Testament book of Job takes us into the life of man, who virtually loses everything in a single day. Job's possessions, livelihood, children and health are all ripped away in tragic circumstances. And Job is crippled by mind-numbing anguish.

On one level, therefore, the book of Job is all about suffering. It offers certain insights into why bad things happen. However it is important to note from the outset that this is not the main focus of the book. As we'll discover, Job isn't really about why suffering happens. It's more about how we should act towards God when suffering happens.

In this respect, Job is much more practical than it is theoretical. It's a bit like a first aid manual. A first aid manual doesn't really go into great detail about all the different reasons why you might break your arm. It's more interested in explaining how to act when your arm is broken. That's like Job. It doesn't give us an exhaustive catalogue of reasons as to why suffering happens. It's more concerned to explain how to act towards God when suffering happens.

Job is a book about whether God is worth following even when we are suffering. It's about whether God is worth trusting even when he seems to be making our life a misery.

But first things first. Let's meet the man Job and discover a bit about him.

Investigate

Read Job 1:1-5
1. What are Job's physical circumstance like?

plentiful

2. What is Job's character like?

blameless + upright

3. Read Proverbs 3:1-8. According to the Proverbs how are Job's wealth and blamelessness linked?

kpg Gs cmmnds —> prosperity + health

Job the man

In these opening verses, we are left in no doubt that Job is a godly man. We especially see it in the way that Job is concerned not just for his own relationship with God, but also for his family. He even makes sacrifices just in case his children have done something silly (Job 1:5). This man is a model of loving concern. He is presented as the perfect example of a godly, wise man.

Job is also astronomically wealthy. He owned 7000 sheep, 3000 camels, 500 yoke of oxen and 500 donkeys. Job is the Bill Gates of ancient Edom.

All of this is exactly what we would expect from the Proverbs. As we've discovered in the above questions, Proverbs predicts that if you "fear the Lord and shun evil" you will be healthy, wealth and wise. Job feared the Lord and shunned evil, and he was wealthy, healthy and wise. So far everything fits perfectly. Everything is as it should be. Everything is as we would want it. A good man enjoying a good life.

But all that is about to change. Some bad things are about to happen to this good man.

Investigate

Read Job 1:6-22.
1. What is Satan's accusation against Job?

2. How does God respond?

3. What do we learn about God and Satan in these verses?

4. What does Satan cause to happen to Job? What different types of events does Satan use to bring suffering to Job?

5. How does Job respond?

Job's first test

In the space of a few minutes, Job loses everything. His wealth, his cattle, his sheep, his camels, his servants, his precious children whom he worried over so much; they are all gone. Ripped away from him by both natural disasters and human violence.

The reason for Job's suffering is revealed to us, the readers, if not to Job. Satan has come before God and questioned Job's righteousness. Satan argues that Job only follows God for what Job can get out of it. According to Satan, Job Is not interested in God at all really. Job just likes the gifts that God gives, and so if the gifts suddenly disappear he will curse God.

In one sense, it is a slur against Job's character, but it is also a slur against God. Satan is suggesting that God can only win friends for himself by giving them things. He is suggesting that God has to buy followers with bribes and prizes.

The story progresses with God accepting Satan's challenge, and it would seem by the end of chapter 1 that Satan has been proved wrong. After losing his prosperity and family, Job does not do what Satan predicted. Just the opposite–rather than curse God, Job praises him.

Satan, however, remains unconvinced.

Investigate

Read Job 2

1. In this chapter what further things do we discover about God, Satan and Job?

a. God

b. Satan

c. Job

2. To what extent does Job understand why he is suffering?

Job's second test

By the end of chapter 2, Job has gone from prosperity to poverty, from great comfort to crippling pain, from being the greatest man among all the people of the East to sitting on a rubbish tip scratching his scabs with a broken piece of pottery.

In all this, it is crucial to notice that Job has not been privy to the discussion between Satan and God. Job knows nothing about what has happened in heaven. Job only knows suffering. Indeed, much of the remainder of the book is taken up with Job arguing with his friends and struggling with God over why these terrible things have happened to him.

For us the reader though, the issue is slightly different. Unlike Job, we do know why he is suffering. We are told in the first eleven verses! Job is suffering as a test of his righteousness. For us, the readers, the real tension of the book is whether or not Job will remain faithful? Will Job's despair cause him to curse God? Will Satan be proved right?

In the studies which follow we will discover how Job handles his sufferings. As we do so, the question which will pop up time and time again is: How should we respond to God when bad things happen to us and we don't understand why?

Think it through

1. When we suffer, do you think it is usually for the same reasons as Job?

2. Satan accuses Job of being more interested in God's gifts than God himself. To what extent could this be true for you? What are some ways that we could ensure we don't fall into that trap?

3. In what ways is God's sovereignty revealed in these opening chapters?

4. When is it hard to believe that God is in control?

5. When we are suffering, how can it be comforting to remember that God is in control?

2

Life is never that simple

"Nothing comes from nothing, nothing ever could. Somewhere in my youth or childhood I must have done something good."

Many of us probably recognize those words from Roger and Hammerstein's, *The Sound of Music.* Do you remember the scene? Maria is back after having run away, all the children are happy again, Captain von Trapp has called off his engagement to the Baroness, and Maria and the Captain have finally declared their love for one another. All is well with the world. Everyone in the audience is feeling warm and fuzzy. And Maria sings that somewhere in her youth or childhood she must have done something good to deserve this moment.

Is that the way life operates? Is that the secret to getting on in the world? That if we do good things, then good things will happen to us; and if we do bad things bad things will happen to us? Is that how it works?

Many of us instinctively think so. When something goes wrong, often our immediate response is, "What have I done to deserve this? Am I being being punished here for something?" In some Christian circles, this sort of thinking is reinforced with very spiritual sounding reasons. People are told that the reason they are sick or in trouble is because they have some unconfessed sin in their life. They are told that if they confess their sin and repent then things will get better.

But is that the way life works? That is the question we'll be investigating in this study.

Investigate

1. **Read Job 2:11-13.** What do Job's three friends do in response to his suffering. What does this tell us about his friends?

2. **Read Job 3.** What does Job say to his friends about his own suffering? How does this compare with what Satan predicted in 2:5?

Job's comforters

In our last study, we left Job sitting in ashes, scratching the scabs that covered his body from head to foot. Three friends of Job now arrive, and at first they are so horrified by what they see that for a whole week they sit in silence. It is Job who breaks the silence with a sad lament of his birth (ch 3). This is all the invitation the friends need to now speak for themselves, and for the next 31 chapters a huge debate develops between Job and his friends, as they argue about why all this has happened to Job.

In one sense, the structure of Job simply mirrors life. In a chapter and a half, Job loses everything, but then for the next 30 chapters there is endless soul searching, grieving, arguing and wondering why. This echoes reality. It can take a five minute phone call to bring your whole life crashing down, but the grieving and confusion can go on for months if not years.

Unfortunately, it is at this stage of the book that many readers lose interest, for as the discussion between Job and his friends develops it becomes somewhat repetitive and (to us) long-winded. The pattern which develops is that Job's three friends each take turns at explaining to Job why it is that he is suffering. After each friend has had their say, Job himself replies to them before the next friend speaks. This entire pattern then repeats itself two more times. All this can be represented by the following table:

Round 1	
Eliphaz speaks	.....Job responds (4-7)
Bildad speaks	.....Job responds (8-10)
Zophar speaks	.....Job responds (11-14)
Round 2	
Eliphaz speaks	.....Job responds (15-17)
Bildad speaks	.....Job responds (18-19)
Zophar speaks	.....Job responds (20-21)
Round 3	
Eliphaz speaks	.....Job responds (22-24)
Bildad speaks	.....Job responds (25-26)
.....Job responds (27)	

It can be seen that the discussion runs out of steam towards the end, with Zophar not even offering a third speech. We'll say more about this later. For the remainder of this study, we will be dipping into some of the things that Job's friends say. We'll wait to consider Job's responses in our next study.

So then, what words of comfort do Job's friends have to offer?

Investigate

1. *Read Eliphaz's first speech in Job 4-5.*

   a. How would you describe the tone of Eliphaz's speech? Is he supportive? cruel? caring? understanding?

b. What does Eliphaz think is the reason behind Job's sufferings? (4:7-8)

c. Why is Eliphaz so confident about his assessment of Job? (4:12-16)

d. What is Eliphaz's advice to Job? (5:8,17)

2. Look now at Eliphaz's last speech in Job 22. Is he still saying the same things?

3. *Read Job 8:1-7.*
    a. What does Bildad think is the reason behind Job's suffering?

    b. What does Bildad think Job should do to restore his blessings?

4. **Read Job 11:1-6.** What is Zophar's assessment of Job?

5. **Read Job 11:13-20.** What does Zophar think Job should do to restore his blessings?

6. Looking back over the advice of Job's three friends:

   a. What do they have in common?

   b. In what ways are they different?

Nothing comes from nothing?

Despite some variations in emphasis, Eliphaz, Bildad and Zophar all agree that Job's suffering is the result of unconfessed sin. God is just, they argue; good people don't have bad things happen to them—therefore, Job must have done something to deserve the trouble he is experiencing. You almost expect Job's three friends to break out into a variation of the song mentioned earlier: "Nothing comes from nothing. Nothing ever could. So somewhere in your youth or childhood, Job, you must have done something wrong."

We will consider Job's responses to his friends in our next study, suffice to say that Job denies their accusations. Job knows of no sin bad enough to warrant the degree of suffering he's going through.

This leads to a great impasse in the debate. Job's friends cannot get Job to confess his sin, and Job cannot convince his friends that there is nothing to confess!

The frustration for us, the readers, is that we know that Job's friends are wrong. Ever since the very first verse of the book we have known that Job is a blameless and upright man who feared God and shunned evil. We've heard it from God's own lips when he was talking to Satan (1:8). What this alerts us to is that suffering can happen to anyone, even to those who don't deserve it. In this fallen world, sometimes even the innocent can suffer.

Job's friends have failed to appreciate this because their theology is too neat, and their view of God too small. Job's friends make the mistake of reducing God to virtually an impersonal system of cause and effect. In their view of the world, good things happen to good people; bad things happen to bad people—simple as that. The result is that, although much of what they say about God is true, it isn't the complete truth about God. In the end their counsel, though well meaning, is both naive and cruel.

Jesus and undeserved suffering

Job alerts us to the reality that undeserved suffering can happen in this life. Although none of us are perfect, bad things can still happen which are not the direct result of some sin we have committed. This of course raises the issue of why God allows this to happen? And as we'll see, this is exactly the question on Job's lips.

However, we must not forget what we discovered in our first study. The book of Job is most interested not in why seemingly undeserved suffering happens, but in how to respond to God when it happens.

In this respect Jesus Christ stands as our supreme example:
For it is commendable if a man bears up under the pain of unjust suffering because he is conscious of God....To this you were called, because Christ suffered for you, leaving you an example that you should follow in his steps. 'He committed no sin and no deceit was found in his mouth'. When they hurled their insults at him, he did not retaliate; when he suffered, he made no threats. Instead he entrusted himself to him who judges justly (1 Pet 2:19-23).

Think it Through

1. What can we learn from Job's friends concerning helping each other through suffering?

2. What do the following passages have to say about the different possible reasons for suffering:

   1 Corinthians 11:27-32

   Hebrews 12:7-11

   Luke 13:1-5

   John 9:1-3

3. Imagine that a friend is going through a great personal tragedy, and someone tells them that their suffering is because of an unconfessed sin their life. What might you say in response to that idea?

4. What do you think it means to "entrust" yourself to "him who judges justly" (1 Pet 2:23)? What practical ways can we help each other do this?

Why me, God?

Late at night on August 31, 1997, Diana, Princess of Wales, was killed in a car accident in Paris. There followed an extraordinary outpouring of emotion around the world. Her funeral was the most watched television event in history, with an estimated world-wide audience of 2.5 billion people. Buckingham Palace and Kensington Palace were awash with an estimated £15 million worth of flowers.

As I sat at home watching all this on television, one particular image stuck in my mind. It was a close up shot of one of the bouquets outside Kensington Palace. Pinned to the flowers was a card with just one word on it. "Why?" That one word seemed to capture so many people's sentiments. Why do things like fatal car accidents happen? Why do beloved people die early in life? Why are young children left without a mother? Why are so many people around the world put through such grief?

Maybe there have been times of suffering in your life when you have asked the same question. "Why?" It is the question that Job asks God throughout Job 3-27.

In our last study we noted that Job 3-27 contains a long and rather repetitive discussion between Job and his three friends, Eliphaz, Bildad and Zophar. Job's friends are convinced that Job's suffering must be the result of some unconfessed sin that lies within Job's life. In this study, we will examine Job's responses to his friends accusations.

Investigate

Read Job's first response to Eliphaz in Job 6-7.

1. How does Job describe his anguish? (6:1-7)

2. What does Job wish would happen to him and why? (6:8-13)

3. How does Job feel about Eliphaz's advice? (6:14-30)

4. How does Job feel towards God? (7:11-21)

Job's answer

In response to his friends accusations, Job insists he has not done anything to warrant his suffering. Job denies that there is some secret sin lurking in his life that has caused his distress. Job is not claiming to be perfect, but simply that he has not done anything bad enough to warrant the degree of suffering he's going through.

This actually puts Job in a very frustrating situation. If Job's friends were correct then his suffering could be more easily managed. It would be a matter of confessing and repenting the sin and then his good fortune would be restored. This is exactly what Elipaz predicts could happen (5:17-27). But it's not that simple for Job. Job knows that there is nothing to confess! All that is left for Job is to mourn the extent of his suffering (6:2-3), beg that God might shorten his life (6:8-9) and struggle over why God would do this to him (7:20-21).

Investigate

1. *Read Job 9:1-20.* What does Job seem to be saying about God here? What is Job's frustration?

2. *Read Job 13:20-27.* What does Job ask of God?

3. *Read Job 19:23-29.* How does Job express his confidence in God's justice?

4. *Read Job 27:1-6.*

    a. What does Job accuse God of doing?

    b. What is Job's attitude to God in these verses?

c. How do Job's responses to his suffering compare with what Satan predicted in 1:11 and 2:5?

4. In Study 2, we discovered that Job's friends had too small a view of God. They treated him as an impersonal cause and effect. Are there any signs of this same attitude in Job?

Job's frustration

In his suffering Job, like us, moves through a wide range of emotions. At times, Job is so confident of God's sense of justice that even if a resurrection from the dead is required to vindicate him, then it would happen (19:25-26)! At other times, Job's despair causes him to question whether God would even give him a fair trial to prove himself (9:14-17). As his bitterness grows, Job's language even drifts into disrespect towards God (27:2-6). We will return to consider this in a later study.

What is very noticeable, however, is Job's frustration at several levels. For starters, Job is in desperate need of a true friend. In 6:14, Job says that, "a despairing man should have the devotion of his friends, even though he forsakes the fear of the Almighty. But my brothers are as undependable as intermittent streams."

Job's suffering is heightened by his loneliness. He desperately needs a friend who will stick by him rather than the "undependable", "intermittent streams" that he presently has for friends (6:14). Better still, Job needs a friend who can empathize with him, someone who knows what it's like to be in his shoes, to suffer great loss for no apparent reason.

As well as a friend, Job admits that he needs an advocate to represent him before God. Job is well aware that God "is not a man like me that I might answer him, that we might confront each other in court. If only there was someone to arbitrate between us, to lay his hand upon us both" (9:32-33).

Job is frustrated that God is so different to us. How on earth can we really relate to the God of the universe? Job sees that he needs an arbitrator and mediator to bridge the gap between us and God.

Job needs a friend and a mediator. It's not too hard to see that Job needs Jesus.

Think it through

1. Think back to a time when you have suffered. How did you feel towards God? In what ways were you similar and different to Job?

2. *Read Hebrews 4:14-16.* Why is Jesus the perfect friend and arbitrator?

3. How would knowing Jesus have helped Job?

4. How does knowing Jesus help us when we suffer?

A word about wisdom

There are few things in the world more irritating than a traffic jam. There you are, sitting in your car going nowhere, achieving nothing.

That's the sort of feeling we have by the time we reach Job 28. The discussion between Job and his friends is going nowhere and seems to be achieving nothing. Job's friends are convinced that his suffering is the result of a secret, unconfessed sin, whereas Job maintains that no such sin exists. Neither side is budging. The discussion has reached a stalemate, so much so that Zophar can't even be bothered contributing to the debate anymore (see the diagram in study 2). No-one is going anywhere.

It's at this point that chapter 28 blows through the book like a breath of fresh air. The chapter comes right in the centre of Job's last speech to his friends. But the chapter doesn't sound like it is Job who is speaking. The language seems almost too calm and objective for Job. And it doesn't sound like any of Job's friends for the same reasons. It's as if chapter 28 is a bit of a break from all the monotonous arguing. It bursts into the book with a fresh perspective which will help us understand the main lesson of the book.

Before we look at Job 28, however, let's recall some connections between Job and wisdom.

Investigate

1. **Read Proverbs 3:1-20.** What does this chapter say about:

    a. the value of wisdom?

    b. the characteristics of a wise person?

    c. the results of a wise life?

2. Look back at Job 1:1-3. In what ways was Job portrayed as the perfect example of a wise man?

The nature of wisdom

It can be seen from Proverbs that when the Bible speaks of 'wisdom, it is referring to something more than academic knowledge. Being wise is not simply being intellectually smart, or getting good marks at school or university. Wisdom is practical knowledge. It is knowing how to get the most out of life. This is because wisdom taps into the principles and patterns of creation (Prov 3:19-20). Wisdom is based on understanding how the world operates (because it is God's world), and therefore how to live best within it.

Let us discover now what Job 28 has to say about wisdom.

Investigate

1. **Read Job 28:1-11.**

   a. What things of value are these verses about?

   b. Where can they be found?

   c. In what ways are man's achievements impressive?

2. **Read Job 28:12-28.**

   a. What thing of value is now being discussed? How does it compare with the precious things discussed in the earlier verses?

   b. Where can it be found? (v. 28)

   c. What does it mean to "fear" the Lord?

The big idea of Job

The climax of Job 28 is that wisdom comes from God. This makes sense. Since it is God who created everything, he more than anyone should know what is wise and what is foolish. Only God can truly know the best way to live within his creation. True wisdom is therefore to fear the Lord (v. 28). In other words the best way to negotiate this life is by living in reverent submission to the One who made us.

Within Job, the importance of true wisdom takes on added dimensions. Coming as it does at the close of a debate about why Job is suffering, Job 28 emphasizes the idea that true wisdom is not a matter of knowing why suffering happens; rather, true wisdom is a matter of knowing the God who knows why suffering happens. The appropriate way to approach suffering is therefore not to seek an explanation for it, but to seek to know God better through the experience. For knowing God is infinitely better than not suffering.

Not only is this the climax of Job 28, it is also the lesson of the entire book of Job. The book revolves around the idea that if we want to live this life to the full, it is not a matter of knowing why things happen; instead it is a matter of knowing the God who knows why things happen. The wise person cannot necessarily explain why everything in life happens, but wise person is in a right relationship with God. This is a critically important lesson which we will return to again and again in our last two studies. It is also a lesson which helps us understand how the book of Job points us forward to Jesus Christ.

Investigate

1. According to 1 Corinthians 1:18-25 what is God's wisdom? How is this different from what Jews and Greeks expect or desire?

2. According to Colossians 2:2-3 where is wisdom and knowledge found?

3. Compare Proverbs 3:19-20 with Colossians 1:15-20. What parallels are there between Jesus Christ and wisdom?

Jesus and wisdom

So far Job has taken us into a fallen world where even the innocent suffer. It has raised the whole question of how we should behave towards God in such a world. Now in chapter 28, we learn that in this world of suffering the most important thing is not to know why we are suffering, but to know and fear God, who is the source of all wisdom. This serves to highlight the importance of Jesus Christ, for it is through Jesus that we can most fully know God.

We have already seen that Jesus is the great biblical example of undeserved suffering (cf. 1 Pet 2:19-23). However, in Jesus, and especially his crucifixion, we also see the supreme example of God's wisdom, for in defiance of all worldly wisdom, God chose to save people and bring them to know himself through the suffering and death of his Son on the cross (1 Cor 1:18-2:10). Through Jesus, we are reconciled to God and enter into the fullness of life as God has intended it (Col 2:9-10). In Christ, we can experience every spiritual blessing (Eph 1:3), and we are able to enter into God's eternal kingdom which will never fade or perish (1 Cor 1:18ff). In Christ, we also have everything we need to know for life and godliness (2 Pet 1:3). These are wonderful truths. When we know Jesus we are at the heart of God's plan and goal for his creation. This is why Jesus Christ is the wisdom of God.

Think it through

1. Job 28 has introduced us to the idea that in this world of suffering the most important thing is not to know why we are suffering, but to know God better while we are suffering. What are some ways in which suffering can help us better know God?

2. In 1 Corinthians 1, Paul refers to Jesus as foolishness to the Greeks and a stumbling block to the Jews. What does he mean by that? In what ways is Jesus still foolishness and a stumbling block to people?

3. If Jesus is the wisdom of God and knowing Jesus is so wonderful, why is it that we often feel the need for more in our lives?

4. What are some practical ways that we can help each other remember the greatness of following Jesus?

5. "Blessed are you when people insult you, persecute you and falsely say all kinds of evil against you because of me" (Matt 5:11). Why do Jesus' words make sense given what we have discovered in this chapter about wisdom, suffering and knowing God?

5

'Brace yourself...'

The courtroom is full of people with anxious looks on their faces. The prosecution and the defence have summed up their cases, and the Judge is about to hand down the decision. The hours of argument are now over. All that's left is to hear the verdict. But what will it be? What will the Judge decide? There's tension in the air.

That is scene that greets us in Job 29-40. Much of Job 1-28 has been taken up in a painstaking argument between Job and his three friends. Job has lost everything but his life, and his friends think that it is because of an unconfessed sin. Job, however, knows this not to be the case. So for chapter after chapter, they have argued with each other, with no clear winner emerging.

But now it's time for the Judge's verdict to be handed down. Now it is time for God himself to enter the debate to give his perspective. Before God speaks, however, the two sides sum up their arguments.

Investigate

1. Job sums up his feelings in chapters 29-31. Read Job 30:15-31 and 31:5-12. How does Job feel about:

   a. his suffering?

b. himself?

c. God?

2. In chapter 32 a new person, Elihu, is now suddenly introduced to us. Elihu serves to sum up the case of Job's friends. *Read Job 32:1-33:12.*

a. What can you discover about who Elihu is?

b. Why hasn't he spoken until now?

c. Why doesn't Elihu let Job's friends summarize their own case?

d. What is Elihu's opinion of Job?

3. Elihu goes on (at considerable length!) to defend God. What are some of things that he says of God in Job 36:1-9 and 37:14-24?

"I rest my case"

The debate which has raged since chapter 3 is over. Each side now rests its case. Job for his part has rehearsed the terrible extent of his suffering, and again explains how perplexed he is that God would do this to him.

On the other side, there is a surprising twist. A young man named Elihu appears out of the blue to enlighten everyone with what he claims is a superior argument (Job 32:14-18). For all his big talk though, Elihu doesn't really say much that is new. He rightfully defends God's righteousness and justice, but he mistakenly assumes that Job is wrong in claiming to have no secret unconfessed sin.

And so now the two cases have been heard and summed up. All that is left is for the Judge to hand down his verdict. Brace yourself!

Investigate

1. God now speaks. To capture the majesty of his words, it is worthwhile reading what he says in full. *Read Job 38-41.*

2. Looking back over God's first speech in chapters 38-40:6.

    a. What does God speak about?

    b. Why do you think God speaks like this?

2. At the conclusion of the first speech, God demands an answer from "the one who accuses God", that is, Job (40:1-2). Job doesn't know what to say, and offers no real answer at all. In response, God then begins a second speech, promising that "I will question you, and you shall answer me" (40:7).

    a. What basic criticism does God make of Job in 40:8-14?

    b. How does the material about the behemoth and the leviathan relate to this basic criticism (see esp. 41:10-11)?.

3. *Read Job's response to God's speech in Job 42:1-5.*

    a. What effect does God's speeches have on Job? (42:1-6)

    b. What exactly do you think Job is repenting of?

    c. What good thing comes out of the way God speaks to Job? (42:5)

God's verdict

After 38 chapters of debate about why Job is suffering, God finally speaks. And the surprising thing is what God doesn't say. God gives no reason whatsoever to Job as to why he is suffering. God does not tell Job anything about the conversation with Satan in chapters 1-2. Indeed, instead of giving answers to Job, God mainly asks questions, a crushing list of questions one after the other, all about nature. Tell me, Job, can you shape the earth? Do you know where darkness lives? Can you move the stars around in the sky? Can you can turn a desert into a grassland with a fall of rain? Can you do this? Can you do that? Do you know this? Can you understand that? Question after question after question.

God's words have the effect of completely humbling Job. The questions remind Job of who is God and who isn't. Job is brought to repentance (42:6).

It is important to realise that Job is not repenting from sins which caused his sufferings. We have known from the opening chapter that it was not as a punishment for sin that Job was afflicted. It is not that his friends were right all along and that there was an unconfessed sin in his life. What then is Job repenting of?

During his long series of questions, God says of the leviathan in 40:10-11: "No-one is fierce enough to hold him. Who then is able to stand against me? Who has a claim against me that I must pay? Everything under heaven belongs to me." In the face of this, Job realises that he has been presumptuous and demanding towards God. He repents of the sin of not handling his suffering in the right way. He is repenting of "obscuring God's counsel", and demanding an explanation from God as if God him owed one.

All this teaches us two very valuable lessons. Firstly, we are alerted to the danger of being too demanding with God. In Christ, we enjoy great intimacy, boldness and confidence with God, but we must be careful not to fall into the trap of therefore taking God casually or flippantly. We must never forget that we are the creatures and he the Creator. We have no right to question his ways, or complain of his judgements. We belong to him, like all of creation; we have no claim against him that he must pay.

Even when we suffer—especially when we suffer—we must remember that perspective. Suffering can be a very crippling experience, and in the middle of pain and grief and loss our world can close in around us. We can become completely engrossed in our own selves and our problems. We can become quite selfish.

But no matter how difficult things may be, it is never an excuse for being disrespectful or presumptuous with God. Certainly, we may pour out our troubles to God, and express to him our confusion and sorrow about why he is doing something. But in our struggles with the hard questions of life, we must never overstep the reverence and awe that God deserves. We need to remember our place. He is the Judge, not us. Job experienced more suffering than most of us could begin to imagine. He lost his family, his livelihood and his health, and yet is was still no excuse for inferring that God was unjust in allowing his suffering. It was no excuse for an attitude that demanded an answer from God as if we are owed one.

But secondly, God's questions to Job show us that God's priority is to restore relationship with Job rather than explain to Job why he is suffering. God is more concerned that Job relate to him properly, and submit to him in all things, than with Job knowing the answer to all things. This relates to the important lesson we discovered in our last study: "The fear of the Lord–that is wisdom" (Job 28:28). The key to wisdom, to making the best of life, is not to know why things happen. The key is to know the God who knows why things happen. That is what God seeks to do with Job. God's speeches have the effect of revealing God to Job. He now sees what God is like, and fears God in a way that he never did before.

Think it through

1. Read the following Bible passages and write down how they provide positive examples of how to relate to God during difficult times.

Psalm 57

Lamentations 3:19-33

Habakkuk 3:17-19

Luke 22:39-46

2. What are some practical things we can do which might help prevent us from becoming embittered when we suffer?

3. How does the picture God presents of himself in chapters 38-41 compare with how he is often spoken of today:

   a. among non-Christians?

   b. among Christians?

4. In Job 42:2, we read that "no plan of yours can be thwarted". How does this help us deal with suffering and relate rightly to God?

6

Faith, Mystery and the meaning of Life...

It's now possible to watch 'interactive' movies. Instead of simply sitting down and passively watching the movie, you are given a remote control device with which you can vote at various points throughout the movie on what you would like to happen next. So at certain critical points in the storyline, you use your remote control to cast a vote as to whether the bad guy gets caught yet, or whether you want the couple to say that they love each other, or whether you want to butler or the maid to be the murderer. Depending on what the majority of people in the audience vote for, the movie goes off in that direction. Only in America!

The voting patterns among audiences at these movies has led to an interesting discovery about human nature. People like happy endings. That's what audience after audience chooses–happy endings. We like it when people live happily ever after.

For this reason, the ending of the book of Job should please many of us.

Investigate

Read Job 42:1-17.

1. What is Job's response to God's speeches?

2. What does Job repent of?

3. What is God's opinion of Job's friends?

4. What exactly did Job's friends get wrong about God?

5. What happens to Job after he prays for his friends? How does his final state compare with how he started the book?

6. How do you feel at the end of the book? Happy? Confused? Surprised?

7. Are there any other things or people which you would like to know more about but which the ending doesn't tell you?

And they all lived happily ever after...

Job has taken us into the world of a man who experiences unimaginable suffering. At the beginning of the book, and unbeknown to the human characters in the story, Satan claims that Job is a selfish man who only follows God for what he can get out of it. So to test Job, God gives Satan permission to make Job's life a misery, a task which Satan performs particularly well. Job loses everything.

It only adds to Job's suffering that he hasn't a clue why any of it has happened to him. Job's friends think they know why. They turn up saying that it's all punishment for an unconfessed sin. But both we, the readers, and Job know that this is not the case. Finally, after what seems to be an endless debate between Job and his friends, God himself appears. God doesn't tell Job why he has suffered, or offer any explanation at all. Rather God reminds Job of who is God and who isn't. God rebukes Job for demanding an answer as if he was owed one.

And so for virtually the entire book, most of us wouldn't swap places with Job for anything. His life is a mess, his children are gone, his health is in tatters, his wife is telling him to curse God and die, his friends are telling him to repent of a sin that he knows hasn't committed, and God himself is hauling Job over the coals for being disrespectful. And at the end of it all Job still doesn't know why is life has been made a misery.

Yet here at the end, half way through the very last chapter, things suddenly turn good just as quickly as they turned bad. Job has another family: seven more sons, three more daughters. No women are more beautiful than his daughters. Job becomes wealthier than he ever was. He gains herds twice the size of what he had. Job himself lives to a ripe old age, seeing his children and their children to the fourth generation. Eventually Job dies, "old and full of years", which is a biblical epitaph reserved for the great ones such as Abraham and David.

So Job goes out with a very happy ending–except, as well as being a happy ending, it's also a little confusing. No reason is given for Job's return to good fortune. Is it a reward because he passed Satan's test? And what about Satan anyway? God tells Job's friends that they have been in the wrong. But what about Satan? He was the one who started all the trouble in the first place! What does God say to him?

What about Elihu also? Elihu was the young fellow who had kept quiet until chapter 32. He doesn't rate a mention here at the end. God speaks to Job and to Job's three friends, but not a word to Elihu. Not a word about Elihu. The book ends without us even being sure who he was!

Job's ending may be happy, but it's also a little frustrating because of all the loose ends still dangling. We wish we were told more—which is exactly the point, because that's what life is like.

Think it through

1. Think back over all the characters in the book. Every character to some extent doesn't know or understand something.

    a. What doesn't Satan understand?

    b. What doesn't Job understand?

    c. What don't Job's friends understand?

    d. What doesn't Elihu understand?

    e. What don't we the readers know by the end of the book?

2. Who in the book is the one person who does know and understand everything?

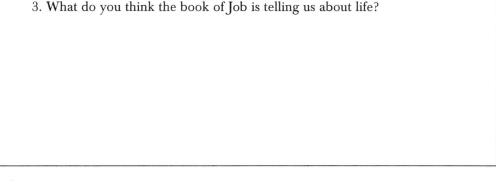

3. What do you think the book of Job is telling us about life?

Life is a mystery

The book of Job is exactly like life. Both the book and life can be confusing and surprising at times. Unexpected bad things can happen. Unexpected good things can happen. Long periods of struggle and anguish and grieving can happen. And there are times in this life when we wish God would tell us more about what is going on.

Job wished God would tell him why he was suffering, but God never does. We wish God would tell us more about Elihu and what happened to Satan at the end. But God doesn't. It's frustrating that he doesn't, but that's just the way life is.

All this mystery only serves to reinforce the main lesson of Job. It is the lesson we learnt in Study 4—that if we want to live this life to the full, it's not a matter of knowing why things happen; it's a matter of knowing the God who knows why things happen.

The book of Job, like life, is full of confusing and surprising and sad and happy times, none of which we may ever fully understand. And the way through it all is not to try to figure out the meaning of every event. That's what Job's friends tried. They wanted to nail everything down and have all the answers. In the end, God condemned their attitude.

No, the wise way to live is not by knowing why everything happens, because we'll never achieve that. The way through the struggles and changes of life is to know the God who knows everything. The way to negotiate life is to know Jesus Christ.

For this reason, when bad or good things happen to us, the main question to grapple with is not, "Why is this happening to me?". The main question to consider is, "Since this is happening to me, how can I use it to know God better through Jesus Christ?".

This is what the book of Job has been about from start to finish. It is about staying close to God, and trusting him, even when bad things happen, because staying close to God is more valuable than not suffering.

Think it through

1. Why is it that we don't value knowing God more than we do? What are some of the things we tend to value more?

2. How we might know Jesus better when:

   a. a personal moral failure occurs?

   b. a tragedy causes great suffering?

   c. we become financially prosperous?

   d. we are in financial trouble?

   e. a close friend fails us?

2. Look back over the studies in this book. Is there any one truth which has stood out to you? Why? What changes are you going to make in your life as a result of this truth?

Tips for leaders

The studies in *The Eye of the Storm,* like all of the Interactive and Topical Bible Studies from Matthias Media, are aimed to fall somewhere between a sermon and a set of plain discussion questions. The idea is to provide a little more direction and information than you would normally see in a set of printed Bible studies, but to maintain an emphasis on personal investigation, thought, discovery and application. We aim to give input and help, without doing all the work for the reader/studier.

Job presents its own particular problems for group Bible study, not the least of which is its length. Especially in the main body of the book (between chapters 3 and 38), there are long passages of discussion and debate which are somewhat daunting. Reading these chapters out in the group may be hard going, and so it is important to encourage the group to read these sections beforehand. Even if the group is not doing any other preparation (more on this below), try to get them to at least read the passages. It will help greatly in picking out what essentially is being said.

In terms of the content of the studies, it is likely that some discussion in the group will focus on God's sovereignty, and how it relates to human responsibility and agency. Some may find it hard to come to terms with the absolute might and rule of God that is represented in Job, but in a sense that is the very point of the final four chapters. You may need to allow extra time to discuss these questions (i.e. after study 5); you may even find that questions of election and predestination emerge as well. It may be worth taking an extra week and doing a topical study on these matters—*The Blueprint* contains a good introductory study on the topic.

The other main issue to be aware of as a group leader is that group members may have differing experiences of suffering—either past or present. For some in the group, the puzzle of Job's sufferings and how to think about it may be largely an intellectual challenge; for others it may represent a very real and personal anguish, given their own very real suffering. You need to be sensitive to this possibility, and respond appropriately (possibly outside the group time).

The studies are designed to work in a group on the assumption that the group members have worked through the material in advance. If this is not happening in your group it will obviously change the way you lead the study.

If the group is preparing...

If all is well, and the group is well-prepared, then reading through all the text, and answering all the questions will be time consuming and probably quite boring. It is not designed to work this way in a group.

The leader needs to go through the study thoroughly in advance and work out how to lead a group discussion using the text and questions as a basis. You should be able to follow the order of the study through pretty much as it is written. But you will need to work out which things you are going to omit, which you are going to glide over quite quickly, and which you are going to concentrate on and perhaps add supplementary discussion questions to.

Obviously, as with all studies, this process of selection and augmentation will be based on what your aims are for this study for your particular group. You need to work out where you want to get to as a main emphasis or teaching point or application point at the end. The material itself will certainly head you in a certain direction, but there will usually be various emphases you can bring out, and a variety of applications to think about.

The slabs of text need to be treated as a resource for discussion, not something to be simply read out. This will mean highlighting portions to talk about, adding supplementary discussion questions and ideas to provoke discussion where you think that would be helpful for your particular group, and so on.

The same is true for the 'investigate' and 'think it through' questions. You need to be selective, according to where you want the whole thing to go. Some questions you will want to do fairly quickly or omit altogether. Others you will want to concentrate on—because they are difficult or because they are crucial or both—and in these cases you may want to add a few questions of your own if you think it would help.

You may also need to add some probing questions of your own if your group is giving too many 'pat' answers, or just reproducing the ideas in the text sections without actually grappling with the biblical text for themselves.

There is room for flexibility. Some groups, for example, read the text and do the 'investigate' questions in advance, but save the 'think it through' questions for the group discussion.

If the group isn't preparing...

This obviously makes the whole thing a lot harder (as with any study). Most of the above still applies. But if your group is not doing much preparation, your role is even more crucial and active. You will have to be even more careful in your selection and emphasis and supplementary questions— you will have to convey the basic content, as well as develop it in the direction of personal application. Reading through the whole study in the group will still be hard going. In your selection, you will probably need to read more sections of text together (selecting the important bits), and will not be able to glide over comprehension questions so easily.

If the group is not preparing, it does make it harder—not impossible, but a good reason for encouraging your group to do at least some preparation.

Conclusion

No set of printed studies can guarantee a good group learning experience. No book can take the place of a well-prepared thoughtful leader who knows where he or she wants to take the group, and guides them gently along that path.

Our Bible Studies aim to be a resource and handbook for that process. They will do a lot of the work for you. All the same, they need to be used not simply followed.

Tony Payne, series editor

Interactive and Topical Bible Studies

Our Interactive Bible Studies (IBS) and Topical Bible Studies (TBS) are a valuable resource to help you keep feeding from God's Word. The IBS series works through passages and books of the Bible; the TBS series pulls together the Bible's teaching on topics, such as money or prayer. As at September 2000, the series contains the following titles:

OLD TESTAMENT

FULL OF PROMISE
(THE BIG PICTURE OF THE O.T.)
Authors: Phil Campbell
& Bryson Smith, 8 studies

BEYOND EDEN
(GENESIS 1-11)
Authors: Phillip Jensen
and Tony Payne, 9 studies

THE ONE AND ONLY
(DEUTERONOMY)
Author: Bryson Smith,
8 studies

FAMINE & FORTUNE
(RUTH)
Authors: Barry Webb &
David Hohne, 4 studies

THE EYE OF THE STORM
(JOB)
Author: Bryson Smith,
6 studies

TWO CITIES
(ISAIAH)
Authors: Andrew Reid and
Karen Morris, 9 studies

KINGDOM OF DREAMS
(DANIEL)
Authors: Andrew Reid and
Karen Morris, 8 studies

BURNING DESIRE
(OBADIAH & MALACHI)
Authors: Phillip Jensen and
Richard Pulley, 6 studies

NEW TESTAMENT

THE GOOD LIVING GUIDE
(MATTHEW 5:1-12)
Authors: Phillip Jensen
and Tony Payne, 9 studies

NEWS OF THE HOUR
(MARK)
Author: Peter Bolt,
10 studies

FREE FOR ALL
(GALATIANS)
Authors: Phillip Jensen
& Kel Richards, 8 studies

WALK THIS WAY
(EPHESIANS)
Author: Bryson Smith,
8 studies

THE COMPLETE CHRISTIAN
(COLOSSIANS)
Authors: Phillip Jensen
and Tony Payne, 8 studies

ALL LIFE IS HERE
(1 TIMOTHY)
Authors: Phillip Jensen
and Greg Clarke, 9 studies

RUN THE RACE
(2 TIMOTHY)
Author: Bryson Smith,
6 studies

THE PATH TO GODLINESS
(TITUS)
Authors: Phillip Jensen
and Tony Payne, 6 studies

THE IMPLANTED WORD
(JAMES)
Authors: Phillip Jensen and
K.R. Birkett, 8 studies

HOMEWARD BOUND
(1 PETER)
Authors: Phillip Jensen and
Tony Payne, 10 studies

ALL YOU NEED TO KNOW
(2 PETER)
Author: Bryson Smith,
6 studies

TOPICAL BIBLE STUDIES

BOLD I APPROACH
(PRAYER)
Author: Tony Payne,
6 studies

CASH VALUES
(MONEY)
Author: Tony Payne,
5 studies

THE BLUEPRINT
(DOCTRINE)
Authors: Phillip Jensen
& Tony Payne, 11 studies

WOMAN OF GOD
Author: Terry Blowes
8 studies

For an up-to date list visit:
www.thegoodbook.co.uk
or call 020-8942-0880